I LOVE YOU TO THE MOON AND BACK

Andrews McMeel
Publishing

Kansas City · Sydney · London

Andrews McMeel Publishing, LLC
an Andrews McMeel Universal company
1130 Walnut Street, Kansas City, Missouri 64106

www.andrewsmcmeel.com

14 15 16 17 18 TEN 10 9 8 7 6 5 4 3 2 1

ISBN: 978-1-4494-6331-1

Library of Congress Control Number: 2014941887

Published by arrangement with Summersdale Publishers Ltd.

To.....................................

From...................................

Love knows not
distance; it hath no
continent; its eyes are
for the stars.

Gilbert Parker

Talk not of wasted affection; affection never was wasted.

Henry Wadsworth Longfellow

Love recognizes no barriers. It jumps hurdles, leaps fences, penetrates walls to arrive at its destination full of hope.

Maya Angelou

We come to love not by finding the perfect person, but by seeing an imperfect person perfectly.

Sam Keen

Love is but the discovery of ourselves in others and the delight in the recognition.

Alexander Smith

Real love stories never have endings.

Richard Bach

Love is ... born with
the pleasure of looking
at each other, it is
fed with the necessity
of seeing each other,
it is concluded with
the impossibility of
separation.

José Martí

O come, and take
from me
The pain of being
deprived of thee!

Thomas Campion

Keep love in your heart…. The consciousness of loving and being loved brings a warmth and richness to life that nothing else can bring.

Oscar Wilde

Mine is the heart at your feet
Here, that must love you to live.

Algernon Charles Swinburne

Love is not love
Which alters when it
alteration finds.

William Shakespeare

If I had a flower for every time I thought of you … I could walk through my garden forever.

Alfred, Lord Tennyson

Ultimately love
is everything.

M. Scott Peck

You are my
only love. You have
me completely in
your power.

James Joyce

The more I think it over, the more I feel that there is nothing more truly artistic than to love people.

Vincent van Gogh

There is never a time or place for true love. It happens accidentally, in a heartbeat.

Sarah Dessen

Thou art to me a delicious torment.

Ralph Waldo Emerson

Nobody has ever measured, not even poets, how much the heart can hold.

Zelda Fitzgerald

You have made
a place in my heart
where I thought there
was no room for
anything else.

Robert Jordan

**No more Thou, and
no more I,
We, and only We!**

Richard Monckton Milnes

The great tragedy of life is not that men perish, but that they cease to love.

W. Somerset Maugham

There is always some madness in love. But there is also always some reason in madness.

Friedrich Nietzsche

He is a heart that strikes a whole octave: after him almost all songs are possible....

Rainer Maria Rilke

Love, like a river,
will cut a new path
whenever it meets
an obstacle.

Crystal Middlemas

One word frees us of
all the weight and pain
of life: that word
is love.

Sophocles

In love the paradox
occurs that two beings
become one and yet
remain two.

Erich Fromm

Love is a temporary madness, it erupts like volcanoes and then subsides.

Louis de Bernières

Let your love be like
the misty rains, coming
softly, but flooding
the river.

Malagasy proverb

Love is in all things a most wonderful teacher.

Charles Dickens

We are all born for love. It is the principle of existence, and its only end.

Benjamin Disraeli

O my Luve's like a red, red rose,
That's newly sprung in June.

Robert Burns

In your light I learn how to love.

Rumi

Life is the flower for which love is the honey.

Victor Hugo

The madness of love
is the greatest of
heaven's blessings.

Plato

If I know what love is,
it is because of you.

Hermann Hesse

A loving heart is the beginning of all knowledge.

Thomas Carlyle

When I saw you I fell
in love. And you smiled
because you knew.

Arrigo Boito

Love vanquishes time.

Mary Parrish

If thou hadst never met mine eye, I had not dreamed a living face Could fancied charms so far outvie.

Anne Brontë

Love is most
nearly itself
When the here
and now cease
to matter.

T. S. Eliot

Anyone can be
passionate, but it takes
real lovers to be silly.

Rose Franken

All love is original,
no matter how many
other people have
loved before.

George Weinberg

**lovers alone
wear sunlight.**

E. E. Cummings

Grow old along
with me!
The best is yet to be.

Robert Browning

My love, my hope,
my all shall be
To look to heaven and
look to thee!

William Winter

The best thing to hold onto in life is each other.

Audrey Hepburn

Love must be as much a light as a flame.

Henry David Thoreau

I want to do with you
what spring does with
cherry trees.

Pablo Neruda

Soul meets soul on lovers' lips.

Percy Bysshe Shelley

Love is a canvas furnished by nature and embroidered by imagination.

Voltaire

Love is friendship set on fire.

Jeremy Taylor

Love possesses not nor would it be possessed; for love is sufficient unto love.

Kahlil Gibran

Eventually you will come to understand that love heals everything, and love is all there is.

Gary Zukav

Love is the condition
in which the happiness
of another person is
essential to your own.

Robert A. Heinlein

Come live in my heart,
and pay no rent.

Samuel Lover

I am in love–and, my
God, it's the greatest
thing that can happen
to a man.

D. H. Lawrence

Love is a game that two can play and both win.

Eva Gabor

A heart that loves is always young.

Greek proverb

We were together—
all else has long been
forgotten by me.

Walt Whitman

In dreams and in love there are no impossibilities.

János Arany

Paradise is always where love dwells.

Jean Paul Richter

If you press me to
say why I loved him, I
can say no more than
because he was he,
and I was I.

Michel de Montaigne

One half of me is yours, the other half yours.

William Shakespeare

Each moment of a
happy lover's hour is
worth an age of dull
and common life.

Aphra Behn

Love gives itself;
it is not bought.

Henry Wadsworth Longfellow

Many are the starrs I see, yet in my eye no starr like thee.

Inscription on an English poesy ring

I love her and
that's the beginning
and end of everything.

F. Scott Fitzgerald

Love does not dominate; it cultivates.

Johann Wolfgang von Goethe

Who, being loved,
is poor?

Oscar Wilde

Nothing we do,
however virtuous, can
be accomplished alone;
therefore, we are
saved by love.

Reinhold Niebuhr

Kiss me and
you will see how
important I am.

Sylvia Plath

You are my heart, my life, my one and only thought.

Arthur Conan Doyle

Love, you know, seeks to make happy rather than to be happy.

Ralph Connor

Bid me love, and
I will give
A loving heart to thee.

Robert Herrick

A flower
cannot blossom
without sunshine,
and man cannot live
without love.

Max Müller

Sometimes the heart sees what is invisible to the eye.

H. Jackson Brown Jr.

With thee conversing I forget all time.

John Milton

Love distills desire
upon the eyes, love
brings bewitching
grace into the heart.

Euripides

Love unlocks doors
and opens windows
that weren't even
there before.

Mignon McLaughlin

So many contradictions, so many conflicting emotions are true, and three words explain them: I love you.

Julie de Lespinasse

The winds were warm
about us, the whole
earth seemed the
wealthier for our love.

Harriet Elizabeth Prescott Spofford

I never saw so
sweet a face
As that I stood before.
My heart has left its
dwelling-place
And can return
no more.

John Clare

To love is to feel one
being in the world at
one with us, our equal
in sin as well as
in virtue.

Emmuska Orczy

Love is the only gold.

Alfred, Lord Tennyson

You know you're in
love when you can't
fall asleep because
reality is finally better
than your dreams.

Dr. Seuss

Love is of all passions the strongest, for it attacks simultaneously the head, the heart, and the senses.

Lao-Tzu

Love cures people–both
the ones who give
it and the ones who
receive it.

Karl Menninger

Then seek not, sweet,
the "If" and "Why"
I love you now
until I die.
For I must love
because I live
And life in me
is what you give.

Christopher Brennan

Love in its essence is spiritual fire.

Emanuel Swedenborg

You must allow
me to tell you how
ardently I admire
and love you.

Jane Austen

Where there is love there is no question.

Albert Einstein

Love conquers all things; let us too surrender to Love.

Virgil

Love is itself the beauty of the soul.

Augustine of Hippo

Love is the master-key
that opens the gates
of happiness.

Oliver Wendell Holmes Sr.

The best and most
beautiful things…
cannot be seen or even
touched. They must be
felt with the heart.

Helen Keller

We love because it's the only true adventure.

Nikki Giovanni

And looking to the
Heaven, that bends
above you,
How oft! I bless the Lot
that made me love you.

Samuel Taylor Coleridge

Love doesn't make the world go 'round. Love is what makes the ride worthwhile.

Franklin P. Jones

And in the convulsive
rapture of a kiss–
Thus doth Love speak.

Ella Wheeler Wilcox

Romance is the glamour which turns the dust of everyday life into a golden haze.

Elinor Glyn

A kiss is a lovely trick
designed by nature to
stop speech when words
become superfluous.

Ingrid Bergman

Love is everything it's cracked up to be.... It really is worth fighting for, being brave for, risking everything for.

Erica Jong

Two souls with but a single thought, Two hearts that beat as one.

Friedrich Halm

It is astonishing how little one feels alone when one loves.

John Bulwer

What force is more potent than love?

Igor Stravinsky

Love can turn a cottage into a golden palace.

German proverb

We love the things we love for what they are.

Robert Frost

Love is the joy of the good, the wonder of the wise, and the amazement of the gods.

Plato

I have spread my
dreams under
your feet;
Tread softly because
you tread on my
dreams.

W. B. Yeats

Love that is not madness is not love.

Pedro Calderón de la Barca

Doubt thou the stars
are fire;
Doubt that the sun
doth move;
Doubt truth to
be a liar;
But never doubt I love.

William Shakespeare

Love is the enchanted dawn of every heart.

Alphonse de Lamartine

The heart has its reasons which reason knows nothing of.

Blaise Pascal

Love is something eternal; the aspect may change, but not the essence.

Vincent van Gogh

I knew it was love, and
I felt it was glory.

Lord Byron

Love has no uttermost, as the stars have no number and the sea no rest.

Eleanor Farjeon

Where love is concerned, too much is not even enough.

Pierre Beaumarchais

Love is composed of a
single soul inhabiting
two bodies.

Aristotle

Love is an indescribable sensation— perhaps a conviction, a sense of certitude.

Joyce Carol Oates

Love is not consolation.
It is light.

Friedrich Nietzsche

Love works magic.
It is the final purpose
Of the world story,
The Amen of the
universe.

Novalis

Everything is clearer when you're in love.

John Lennon

There is no disguise
that can for long
conceal love where it
exists or simulate it
where it does not.

François de La Rochefoucauld

Love is being
stupid together.

Paul Valéry

The greatest happiness of life is the conviction that we are loved– loved for ourselves, or rather, loved in spite of ourselves.

Victor Hugo

Where there is great love there are always miracles.

Willa Cather

Love is like the wind; you can't see it but you can feel it.

Nicholas Sparks

One does not fall "in" or "out" of love. One grows in love.

Leo Buscaglia

The consciousness of
loving and being loved
brings a warmth and
richness to life that
nothing else can bring.

Oscar Wilde

One is loved because one is loved. No reason is needed for loving.

Paulo Coelho

At the touch of love
everyone becomes
a poet.

Plato

But we loved with a love that was more than love.

Edgar Allan Poe

In our life there is a single color ... which provides the meaning of life and art. It is the color of love.

Marc Chagall

How do I love thee?
Let me count the ways.
I love thee to the depth
and breadth and height
My soul can reach.

Elizabeth Barrett Browning

But to see her was
to love her,
Love but her, and
love forever.

Robert Burns

Where there is love there is life.

Anonymous

i carry your heart with me(i carry it in my heart)

E. E. Cummings

There is no remedy for love but to love more.

Henry David Thoreau

To love and be loved is to feel the sun from both sides.

David Viscott

Love … must always create sunshine, filling the hearts so full of radiance, that it overflows upon the outward world.

Nathaniel Hawthorne

All mankind love
a lover.

Ralph Waldo Emerson

Harmony is pure love,
for love is complete
agreement.

Lope de Vega

Gravitation is not responsible for people falling in love.

Albert Einstein

Do all things with love.

Og Mandino

I love thee–I love thee!
'Tis all that I can say;
It is my vision in
the night,
My dreaming in
the day.

Thomas Hood

**Love consists in this,
that two solitudes
protect and touch and
greet each other.**

Rainer Maria Rilke

Love comforteth like
sunshine after rain.

William Shakespeare

Two people in love, alone, isolated from the world, that's very beautiful.

Milan Kundera

Love is a beautiful dream.

William Sharp

True love begins when nothing is looked for in return.

Antoine de Saint-Exupéry

I will make a palace fit
for you and me,
Of green days in
forests and blue days
at sea.

Robert Louis Stevenson

The most powerful weapon on earth is the human soul on fire.

Ferdinand Foch

To love abundantly is to live abundantly, and to love forever is to live forever.

Henry Drummond

The sea hath its pearls
The heaven hath
its stars;
But my heart,
my heart,
My heart hath its love.

Heinrich Heine

Love isn't something you find. Love is something that finds you.

Anonymous

If ever two were one, then surely we.

Anne Bradstreet

If you're interested in learning more about our books, find us on Facebook at **Andrews McMeel Publishing** and follow us on Twitter: **@AndrewsMcMeel**.

www.andrewsmcmeel.com